THE TEMPEST LULLABY

THE TEMPEST LULLABY

& Other Poems, Limericks and Riddles

The Bard named Blythe

Acknowledgements

For those who made time to support me,
I now, with this moment, address thee—
Whether help big and small,
My "thanks" goes to all
Who walked with me on this long journey.

CONTENTS

POEMS

The Tempest Lullaby

A stormy night with lightning bright
Will make it hard to sleep—
And lullabies cannot be heard
With thunder in the deep.

But wind and rain will howl in vein,
Once pillow cradles head—
For sleeping is the melody
That puts a storm to bed.

THE BLADE OF GRASS

A blade of grass awoke and said,
"It all belongs to me—
The gleaming light and lovely warmth
Will help me grow, you see?"

And then a little weed replied,
"But it belongs to none!—
So why cannot we all enjoy
The rising morning sun?"

The blade of grass then looked around
At plants and flowers tall,
"Will I enjoy the sun—" he frowned,
"By sharing with you all?"

"Dear friend!—" the little weed replied,
"You need not make a fuss—
The sunlight shines no less on you
When shining too on us!"

THE BEAR

Within the forest deep there lived
The tallest bear around—
But fruit within the tallest trees
He throws upon the ground.

"My favorite food is fruit," he says,
When reaching up a tree—
"But those who cannot reach this high
Love fruit as much as me!"

THE DANCING ELVES

• 16 •

The woodland dells are filled with elves
Who twirl and dance to verse—
And elves will live forever, so
Forever they rehearse.

They tried to comfort me one day,
For dances I knew few—
"A thousand years ago—" they laughed,
"We had to learn like you!"

THE PAINTER

• 18 •

A painter sat but knew not what
His painting was to be—
"Perhaps a dog and cat," he thought,
"Or maybe just a tree."

But still with no decision made
And new ideas faint,
He chose to paint a painter who
Knew not what he would paint!

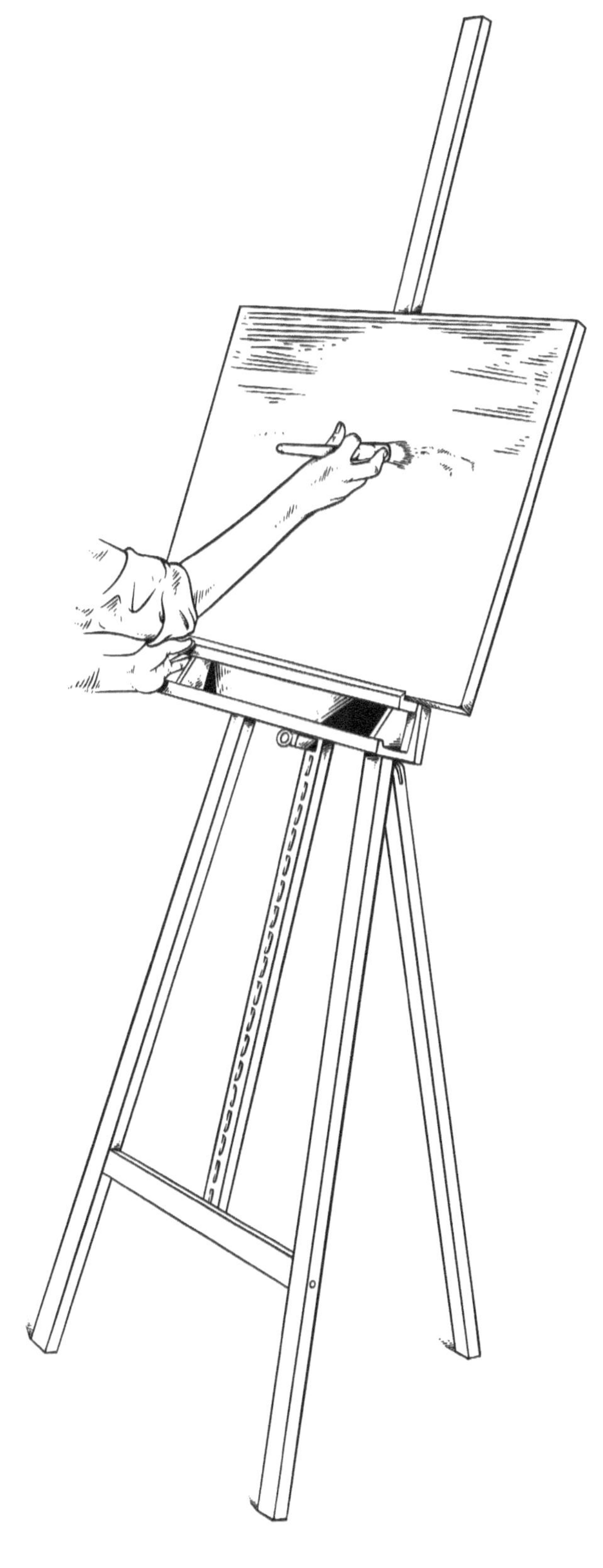

THE TROLL

There lived a troll beneath a bridge
Along the meadowed way—
"Why dwell in such a nasty place?"
I asked him there one day.

"I like it here!—" He laughed aloud,
Without a care to give—
"Why dwell up there where people judge
How other people live?"

The Fire and the Fox

A camping fire in the woods
Was left to burn alone—
And though its flames had disappeared
Its embers were aglown.

A fox had wandered from the dark
And found the fire bright—
Then laid beside the embers' warmth
Throughout the autumn night.

Her slumber in the twilight was
Her warmest evening yet—
But she had not a thing to give,
And that made her upset.

"You come with naught—" the fire said,
"And still my embers burn—
For all my friendship asks of you
Is friendship in return."

THE TULIP

• 24 •

I drew a blooming tulip once
With colors green and pink—
And very special was this plant,
For it could talk and think.

It looked at me and thanked me for
Its lovely leaves and stem,
"But who drew you?—" it wondered still,
"And who—or what—drew them?"

THE WIZARD

A wizard came upon an tree
Whose branches bore a pear—
He casted every spell he knew
To get the tree to share.

"Your wand is useless!" laughed the tree
While swaying with the breeze,
"Alas, the only spells you need
Are manners and a 'please!'"

The Butterfly

I want to find an animal,
One new to you and me—
"A unicorn—" I said aloud,
"Or mermaids in the sea."

A butterfly then fluttered by,
And landed on my ear—
"Be careful not to miss—" it said,
"The world already here!"

THE ZEBRA

A zebra did not like his stripes,
He wanted spots instead—
"I look like all of you—" He frowned,
"The same from tail to head."

"Baloney!" said his friend, "You are
The kindest through and through!—
The rarest zebra, you are not,
Yet still the rarest 'you!'"

THE GNOME

I walked across a hungry gnome
Who asked to share my bread—
"Well half is for my friend," I frowned,
"So take my piece instead."

"Keep your little piece," he laughed,
"'Tis more than I could eat—
Your kindliness has filled me more
Than all the autumn's wheat!"

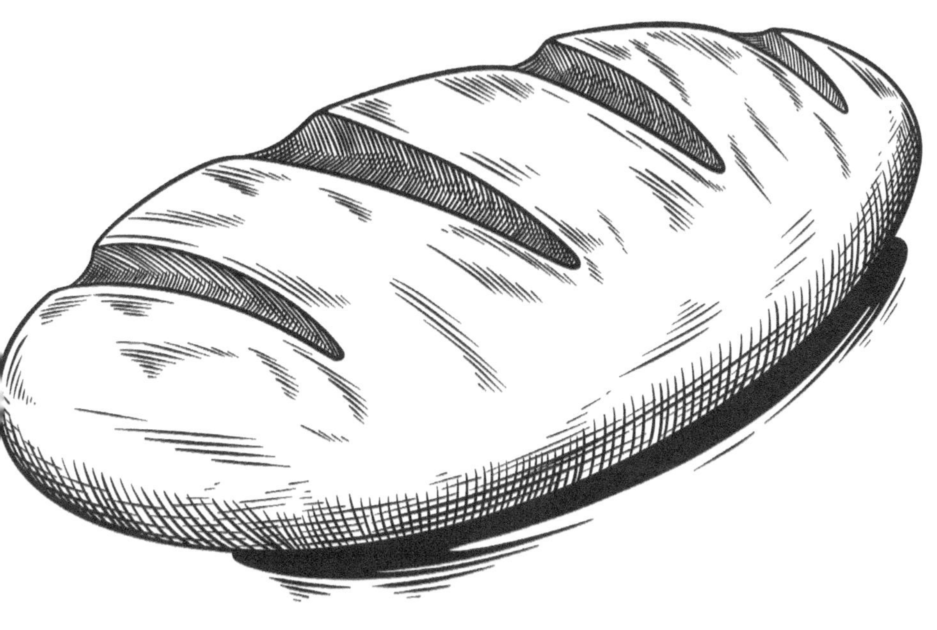

THE LEGEND OF THE LYE

They say the Lye live in the woods,
They say the Lye are mean—
They say, "the Lye are dangerous,
Avoid them if they're seen."

So once upon an autumn's dawn
I went to have a look—
But then I tripped upon a log,
And fell into a brook.

They found me in the water there,
And saw my dampened frown—
"Come with us to dance!" they said,
"Before the sun goes down!"

We danced around a fire bright
Until my clothes were dry—
I say, no more will I believe
The legend of the Lye.

LIMERICKS

THE SMELL

· 38 ·

Today I had smelled something rotten—
A smell that will not be forgotten—
It turned out my dog
Had swallowed a frog,
And terrible had her breath gotten!

THE SOUND

I heard a sound soft as a mumble—
Then turn to an elephant rumble—
I blushed red because
I knew what it was—
My tummy was loudly agrumble!

ANOTHER SOUND

• 42 •

I thought I heard kangaroos jumping,
Or maybe just thunder clouds bumping—
But then I thought, "Gee!—
My dog has to pee!"
For on the floor was her tail thumping!

THE SPRITE

"If only you did more than squeak—"
I said to a sprite by the creek,
It widened its eyes,
And said in surprise,
"Who knew that you humans could speak!"

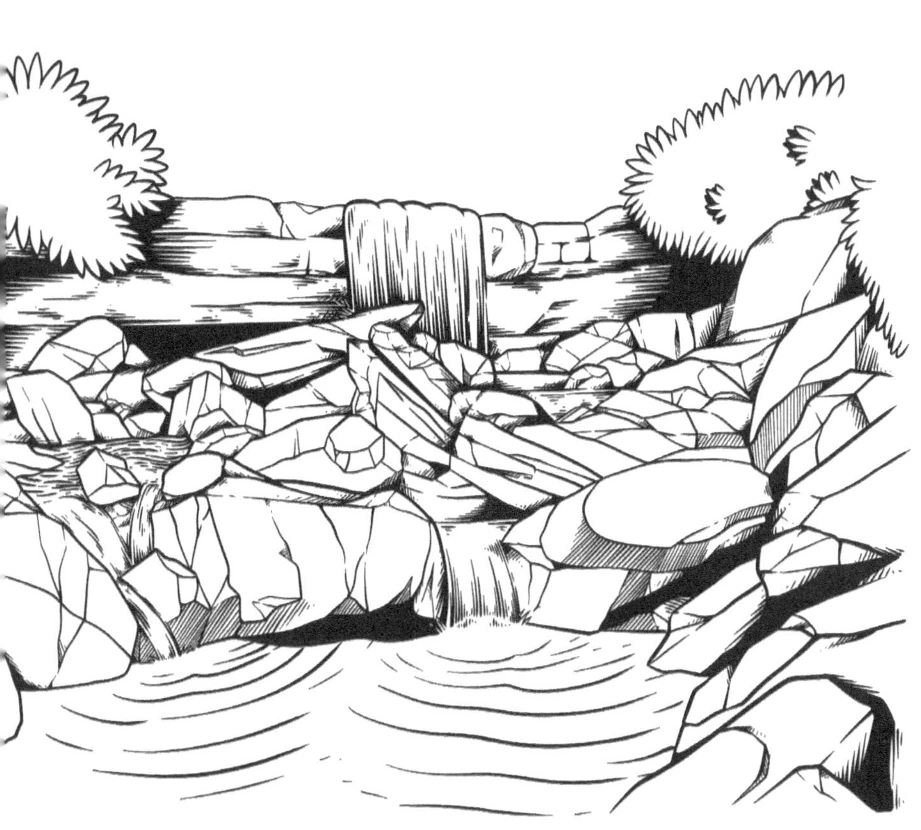

THE ELF

I had bent over low to say "hi!"
To an elf who was standing close by—
"Though short is my spine,
My hearing is fine!"
He declared in his grumpy reply.

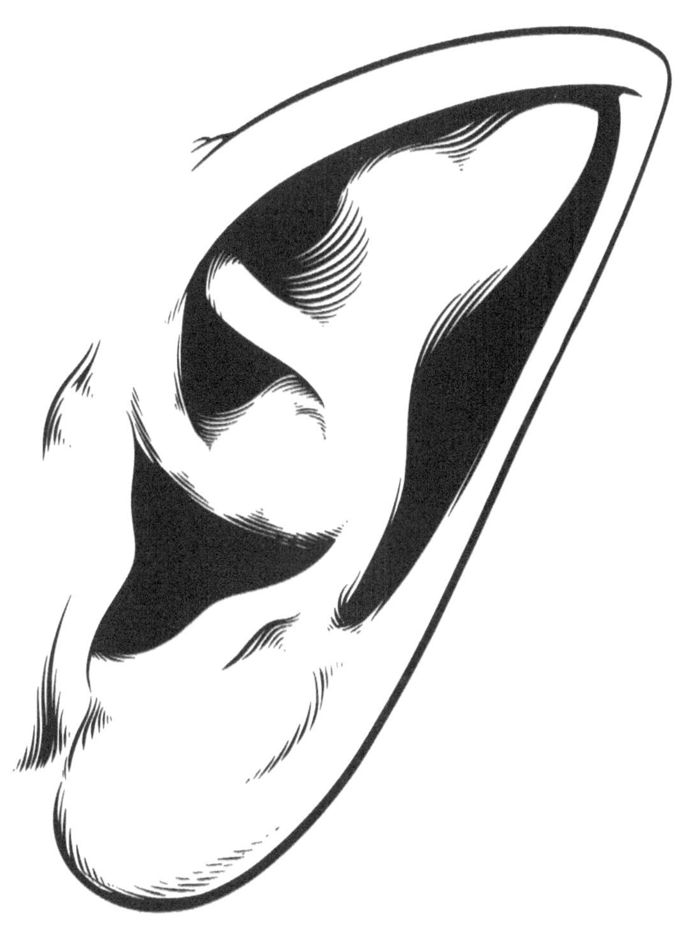

RIDDLES

Riddle I

A blade that cannot cut or slice,
But sharp enough the same—
A blade that will not blunt or dull,
And forged without a flame.

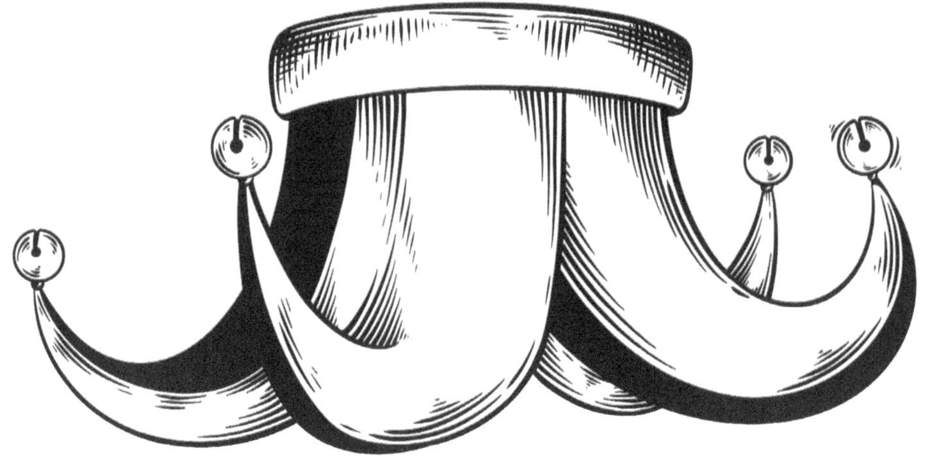

A Blade of Grass

RIDDLE II

• 52 •

I have no eyes but ever wink
At all who meets my gaze—
But you will never see my face
On bright and sunny days.

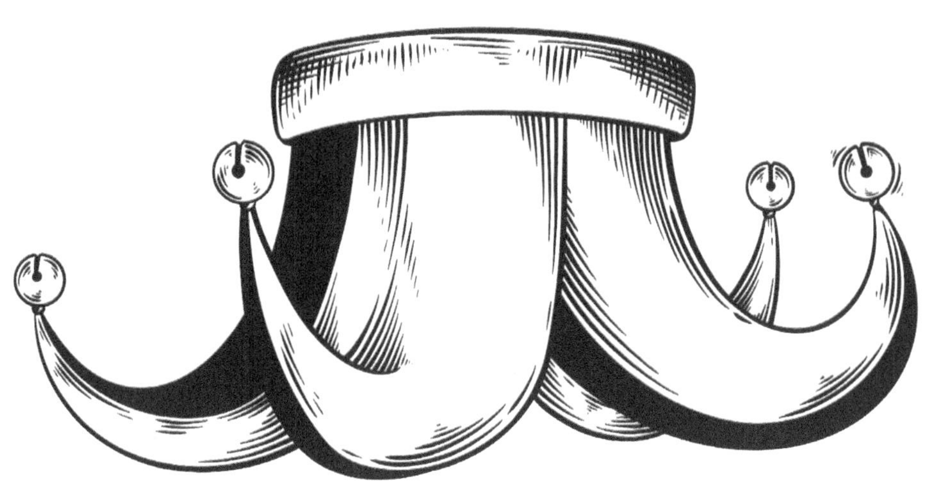

The Night Sky

RIDDLE III

Forever dirty yet cannot
Be filthy or unclean—
And even if you wash me well,
I will not glint or glean.

Dirt

RIDDLE IV

Although I have not legs or arms,
I dance all night and day—
And once I start, I never stop
Until I go away.

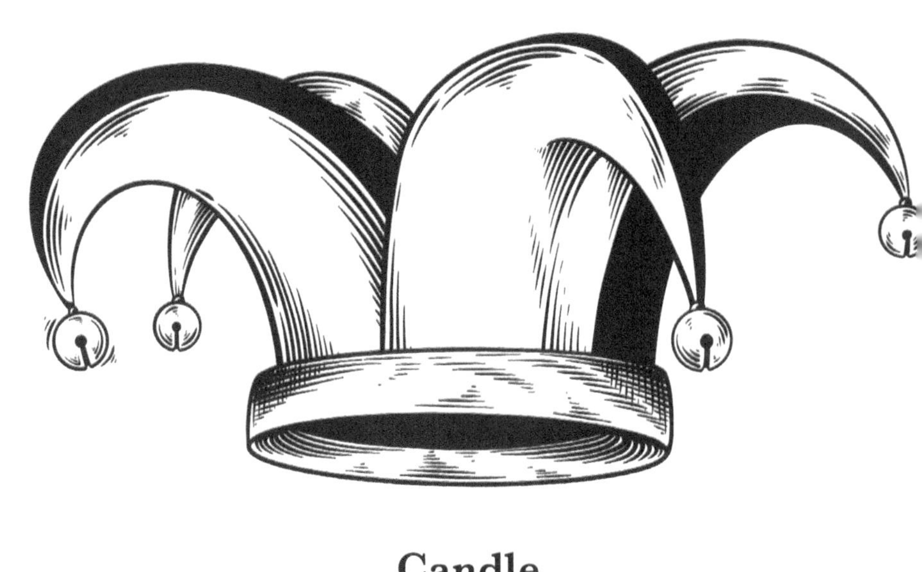

Candle

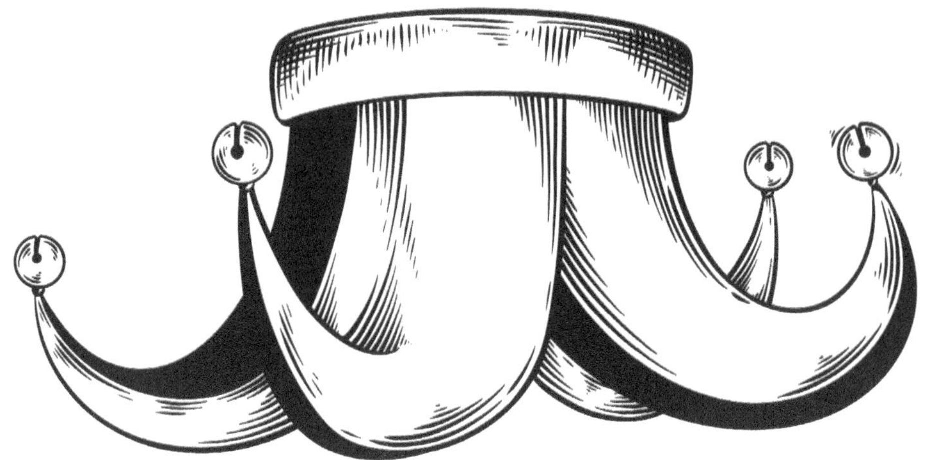

Riddle V

• 58 •

Although we look like other balls,
We cannot roll around—
Still, up and down we bounce, and yet
Will never touch the ground.

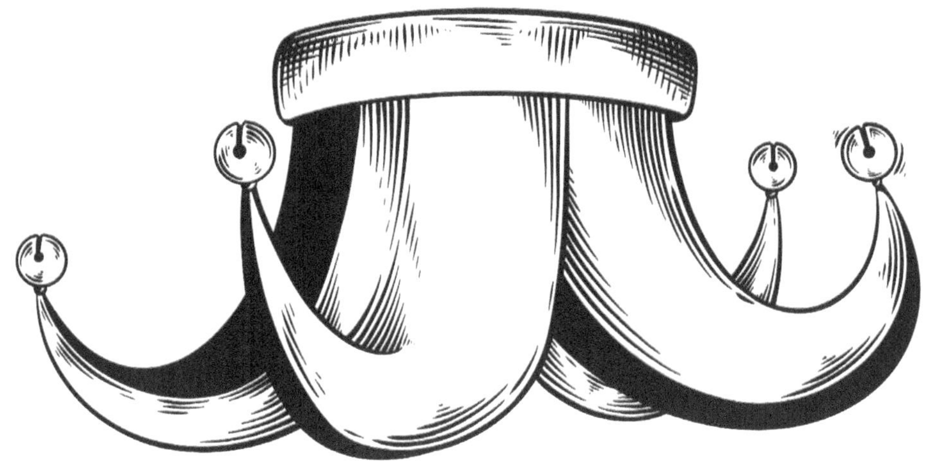

The Sun and Moon

RIDDLE VI

• 6 •

A fairy-story I am not,
But tell of distant lands—
I am a wordless page you read,
And hold within your hands.

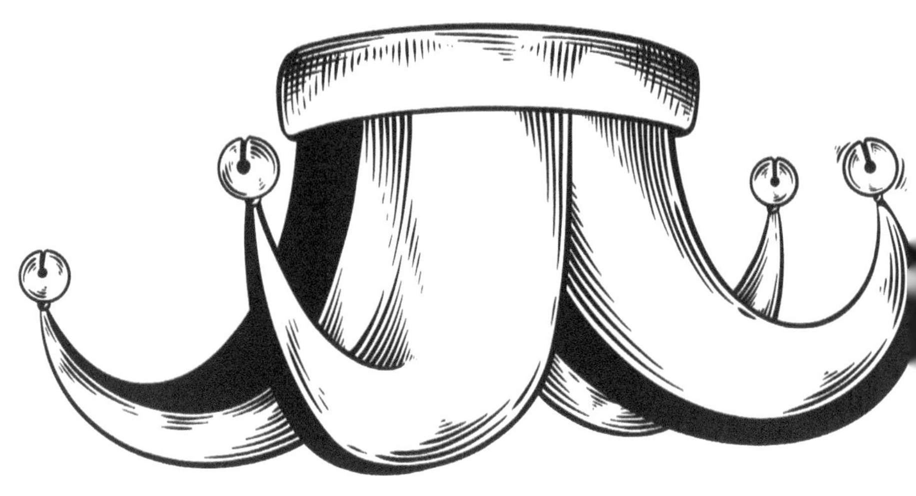

A Map

RIDDLE VII

This key, without a shape of size,
Cannot unlock a door—
And sometimes you may use it once,
And sometimes maybe more.

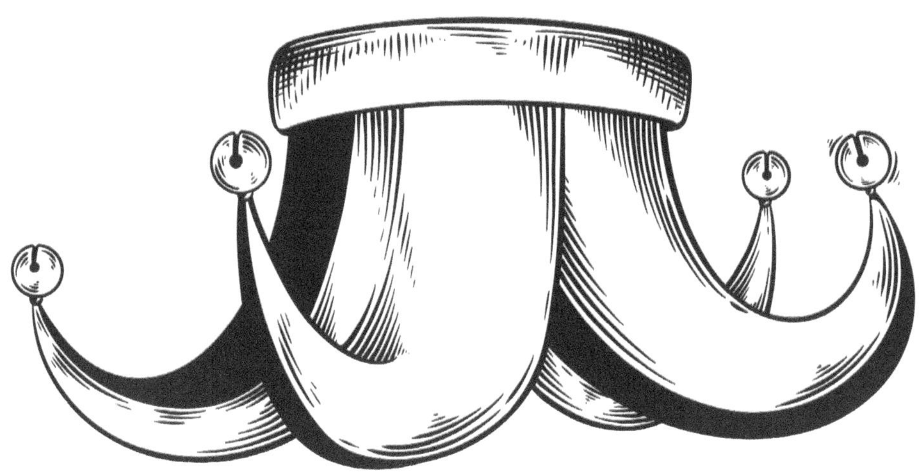

Invitation

Riddle VIII

Too far for you to touch, and yet
So close you see me clear—
But once I reach your mouth or hands,
At once I disappear.

Thought

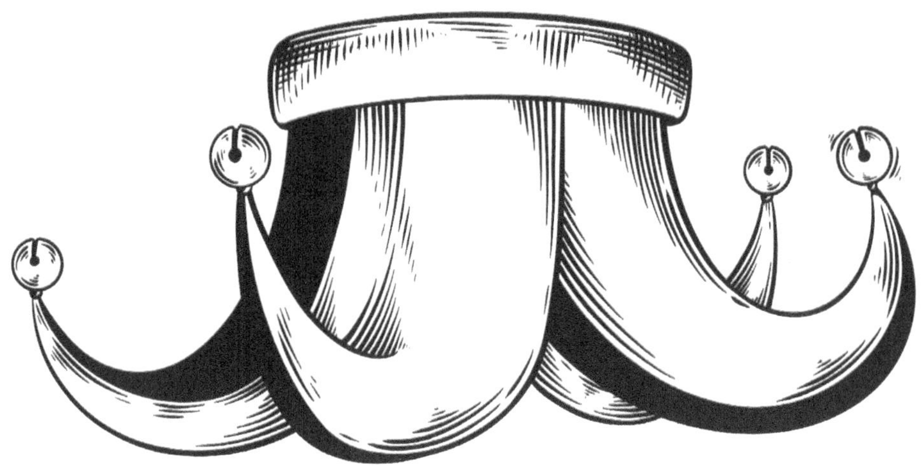

Riddle IX

• 66 •

A smile summons me at once,
Like sun will summon day—
But frowning, on the other hand,
Will send me on my way.

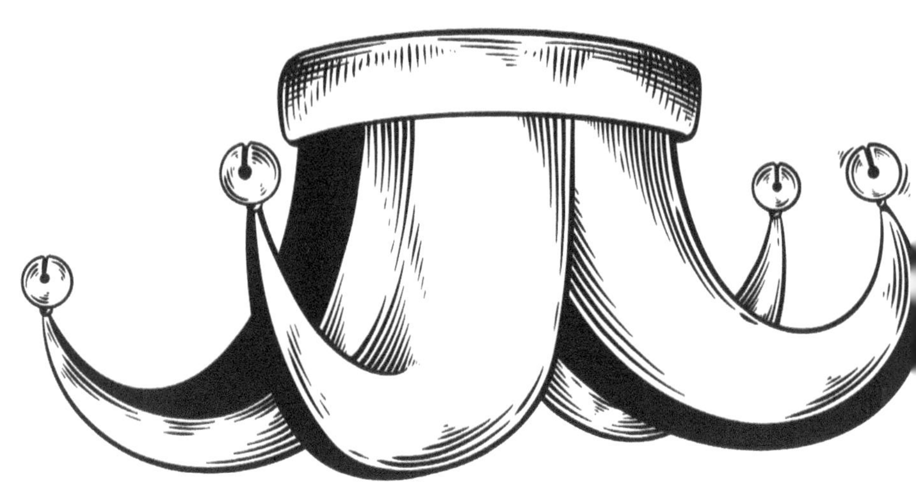

Laughter

Riddle X

Your muscles will not help you for
I'm held by weak and strong—
And even if you hold me tight,
You will not hold me long.

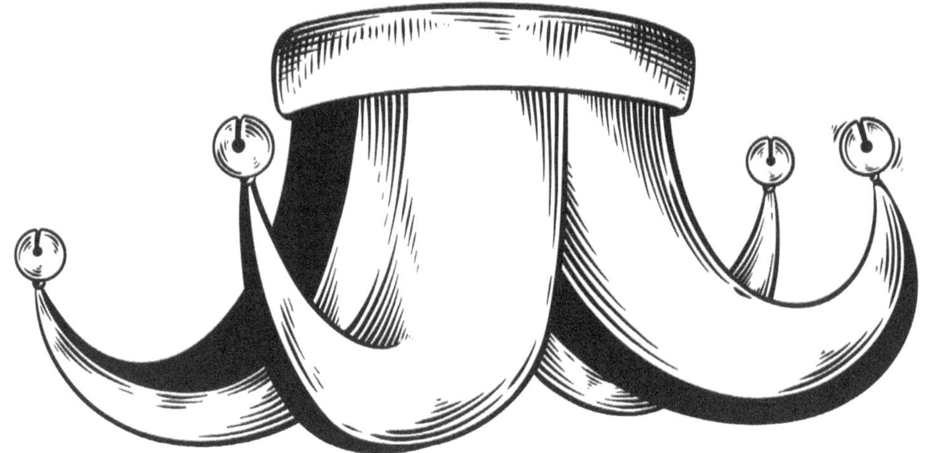

Breath

RIDDLE XI

I can take on any form,
From insects to the sun—
And though I can be any thing,
I'm made of only one.

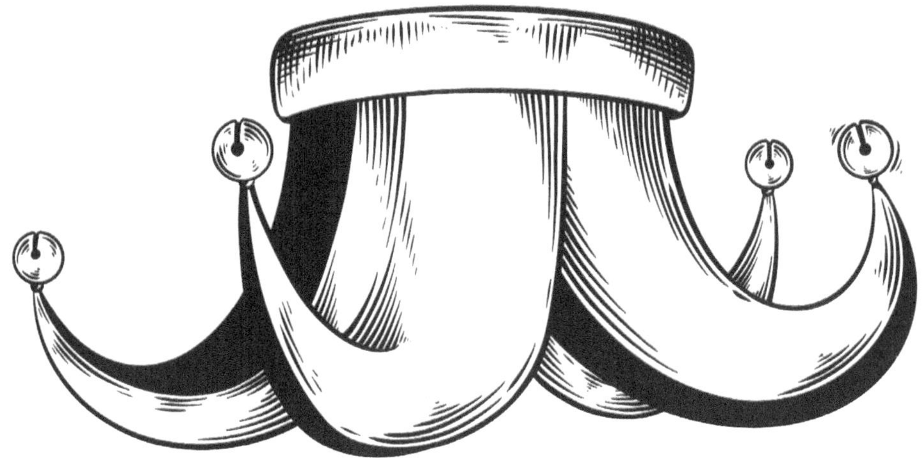

Picture/Painting

Riddle XII

You think of me from time to time,
And won't forget me fast—
And yet the most you'll know of me
Is when you thought me last.

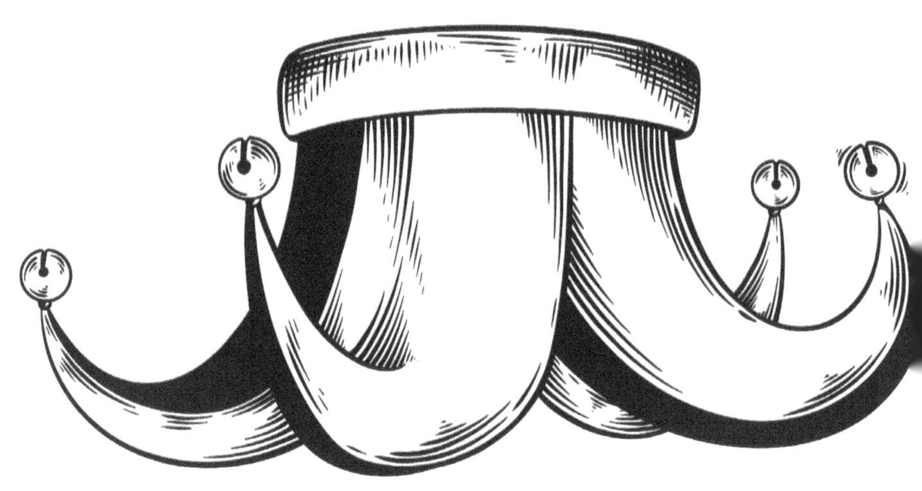

Memory

Riddle XIII

• 74 •

I walk, I run, I jump with fun,
But never make a sound—
I stand about as tall as you
But closer to the ground.

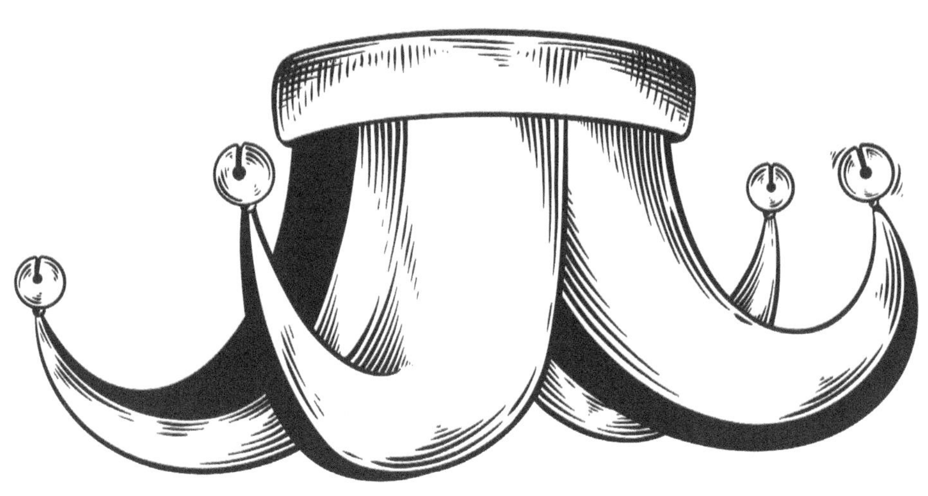

Shadow

The End